LEGO CHIMA

HEROES' QUEST

WRITTEN BY
HEATHER SEABROOK

LONDON, NEW YORK, MUNICH,
MELBOURNE and DELHI

DK LONDON
Senior Editor Sadie Smith
Pre-Production Producer Marc Staples
Producer Louise Minihane
Managing Editor Elizabeth Dowsett
Design Manager Ron Stobbart
Publishing Manager Julie Ferris
Publishing Director Simon Beecroft

DK DELHI
Assistant Editor Gaurav Joshi
Assistant Art Editor Pranika Jain
Art Editor Divya Jain
Deputy Managing Editor Chitra Subramanyam
Deputy Managing Art Editor Neha Ahuja
DTP Designer Umesh Singh Rawat
Senior DTP Designer Jagtar Singh
Pre-Production Manager Sunil Sharma

Reading Consultant
Maureen Fernandes

First published in Great Britain by
Dorling Kindersley Limited
80 Strand, London, WC2R 0RL
A Penguin Random House Company

10 9 8 7 6 5 4 3 2 1
001–196550–Apr/14

A CIP catalogue record for this book is
available from the British Library.

ISBN: 978-1-40934-758-3

Colour reproduction by Alta Image
Printed and bound in China by South China

Discover more at
www.dk.com
www.LEGO.com

Contents

Trouble in Chima™!

The beautiful kingdom of Chima™ is home to special animal tribes who can walk and talk like people. They get their powers from a Sacred Pool full of an energy source called CHI.

But there is trouble in the land of Chima, and the tribes are worried. The water has stopped flowing from Mount Cavora and the Sacred Pool has dried up. The tribes believe that the mythical creatures called Legend Beasts can restart the waterfalls and save Chima.

The Legend Beasts are animals who did not drink from the Sacred Pool. They walk on four legs and are like normal animals, but giant in size.

CHIMA

Heroes Wanted

Special Correspondent

Chima is facing a crisis. The CHI-filled waters of Mount Cavora have stopped flowing. Black smoke from the Outlands has covered the mountain.

A very worried King LaGravis gave *Chima Times* an update on the situation.

> 66 We need brave heroes from every tribe. The only way to deal with this problem is to face it together and with courage. 99
> – King LaGravis

He said, "We have very little CHI left and we are not sure how long it will last. The land will soon wither and our vehicles could run out of fuel."

Chima's only hope are the Legend Beasts who are somewhere in the scary Outlands. King LaGravis is looking for a team of brave heroes to travel to the Outlands to find the Legend Beasts.

TIMES

IN CHI WE TRUST

CHIMA NEEDS YOU!

Are you brave enough to travel to the dangerous Outlands?

VISIT THE LION TEMPLE FOR MORE DETAILS

Band of Heroes

The tribes of Chima used to fight each other over CHI. Now that somebody is trying to take it away from them, they realise that they must join together.

The tribes have chosen their bravest animals to form a band of heroes.

They include: Eris the Eagle, Gorzan the Gorilla, Rogon the Rhino, Laval the Lion, Cragger the Crocodile and Worriz the Wolf.

Together they must travel through the dangerous Outlands jungle in order to find the Legend Beasts.

Laval the Lion

Laval is the son of King LaGravis. He loves to have fun and is eager for adventure. Laval is also headstrong and has a lot to learn. One day he will lead the Lion Tribe and rule over the land of Chima.

Laval thinks he is ready to face the crisis in Chima. He wants to prove to his father that he can be responsible and brave. The journey into the Outlands will be full of danger, but Laval knows that the heroes must be fearless and find the mysterious Legend Beasts.

Cragger the Crocodile

Cragger is very stubborn and does not like to follow rules. He thinks he knows more than everyone else. Above all he likes to win!

Cragger was once Laval's best friend, but now they are enemies. They had a big fight after Cragger used CHI when he was not allowed. Secretly, Cragger misses his friendship with Laval.

Now that Chima is in trouble Cragger must work with Laval to bring back CHI to the Sacred Pool. Perhaps this is the chance for them to become friends once again.

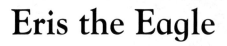

Eris the Eagle

Eris is from the Eagle Tribe
and is the daughter of one
of the many ruling Eagles.
She is very clever and loves
adventures and puzzles.

Eris is a good friend and
always helps others. She is
very fond of Rogon the Rhino.
In battle, Eris uses her brains to work
out a peaceful way to win rather than
fighting. Eris is a very useful member
of the brave team of heroes.

Worriz the Wolf

Worriz is from the Wolf Tribe. He is ruthless and cunning, and always puts himself and his Tribe first.

The Wolves do not get along with the other Tribes, but they must send one of their own to help save Chima. Worriz has been chosen to join the band of heroes. He will travel with the other heroes through the scary Outlands to find the Legend Beasts.

Even though Worriz has never met the Wolf Legend Beast, he loves him. He is determined to find the beast, no matter what it takes.

Rogon the Rhino

Rogon, like the rest of the Rhino Tribe, can be a little stupid. He likes to have fun and is a bit of a party animal.

Rogon does not really understand what the mission is about and why they have to go. But he is coming along for the fun!

However, Rogon is very strong and is good to have on your side – especially when he uses his powerful Rammer Slammer against the enemy!

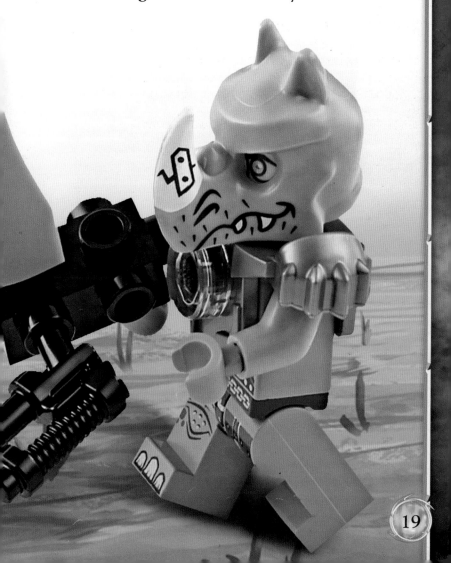

Gorzan the Gorilla

Gorzan is very laidback and sensitive, like most Gorillas. He cares about little things like flowers and insects. Even while fighting he cannot stop worrying about the poor little flowers that he may have stepped on.

Gorzan is a strong and powerful fighter. When he gets angry, he can be a very scary opponent for even the strongest of the Outland Tribes.

WEAPONS

All six heroes are armed with their own highly specialised and advanced weapons. These mighty weapons are powered by CHI, which makes them stronger and more powerful. The heroes must use these special fighting tools if they want to defeat their enemies.

ROYAL VALIOUS SWORD

BELONGS TO: Laval

DESCRIPTION: The Royal Valious Sword was once silver, but now it is black. Laval also has a new Royal Shield and it is super-strong. It protects Laval during an attack.

BLADE BLASTER

BELONGS TO: Cragger

DESCRIPTION: The Blade Blaster has two barrels. It fires out powerful beams of energy. Two sharp sword blades sticking out from either side give added protection.

DERIMOUS SWORD

BELONGS TO: Worriz

DESCRIPTION: The weapons of Chima villains glow red. Now that Worriz has joined the good guys, his Derimous Sword glows a sparkling blue.

BANANA BUSTER

BELONGS TO: Gorzan

DESCRIPTION: The Banana Buster has a giant fist that pops out on a spring. It is also fitted with bananas because, well, Gorzan likes bananas.

RAMMER SLAMMER

BELONGS TO: Rogon

DESCRIPTION: The Rammer Slammer is a very strong weapon for battering down walls. The enemies had better watch out for that pointed Rhino horn.

BOBLADE

BELONGS TO: Eris

DESCRIPTION: Eris's BoBlade has golden wings, which gives it a royal look. However, it can do some serious damage to the enemies.

Dear Dad,

Our band of heroes has reached the Outlands. It is a dangerous place. We have to be careful of the predator plants, which will eat us alive given the chance. They are very tall and the flowers have rows of sharp teeth. Whipper vines are long plants with sharp spikes on the end, which whip at us, trying to pull us into their mouths. Strangler grass grows very fast and tries to suffocate us. There are also poisonous frogs.

Our band of heroes travels fast
through these jungles, but Rogon is
slowing us down with his rock-
filled RhinoTruck.

There is a black cloud filled with
bats, which keeps attacking us, too.

We WILL keep going in the hope
of finding the Legend Beasts and
returning the
CHI to
Chima.
Yours,
Laval

Lavertus the Lion

Lavertus is an outlaw of the Lion Tribe. He was banished to live in the Outlands after an argument with King LaGravis.

Lavertus lives in a place called the "Lair" – a home he has built himself. He flies a special helicopter vehicle called the WindShadow. He is very good at building things!

Lavertus welcomes the heroes on their arrival in the Outlands and offers to help them on their mission.

He uses special tools to improve their weapons, and builds new armour for everyone. The heroes have made an important new friend.

LAVERTUS'S LAIR

A periscope allows Lavertus to spot intruders

Deadly defensive weaponry

Plants camouflage the lair in its surroundings

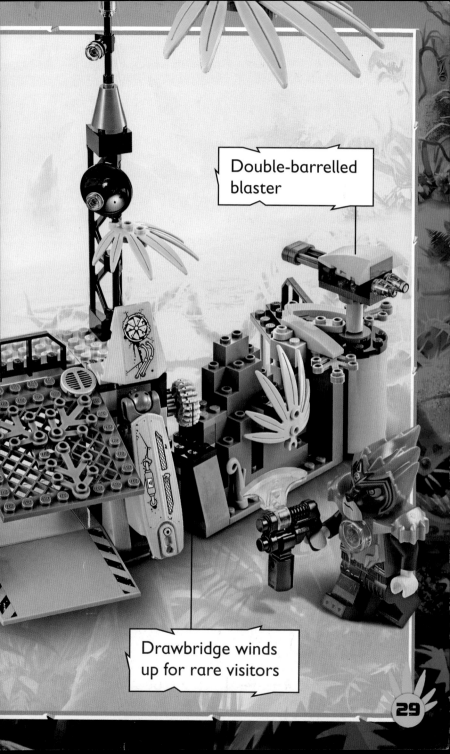

Double-barrelled blaster

Drawbridge winds up for rare visitors

The Spider Tribe

The Spider Tribe lives in the Outlands. They are the cleverest of all the Outland Tribes.

The spiders are very good at building webs and traps. They can use the webs to capture their enemies.

Once the spiders even used their sticky webs to block the waterfalls of Mount Cavora.

The tribe is ruled over by Spinlyn, the very vain spider queen. She looks hideous to every other creature except other spiders. The queen has many spider soldiers at her service.

The Arachnaught

The Arachnaught is a big battle
vehicle that walks on eight
mechanical spider legs. It shoots
out fully formed webs as well as
streams of webbing. The webs
trap enemies and tangle them up,
and the streams of webbing knock
them off their feet.

   The Arachnaught looks scary
with its glowing red eyes and
sharp spider fangs. It even
has a weapons holder
underneath its body.
The Arachnaught's
powerful stomping front
legs are a match for even the
strongest and biggest hero.

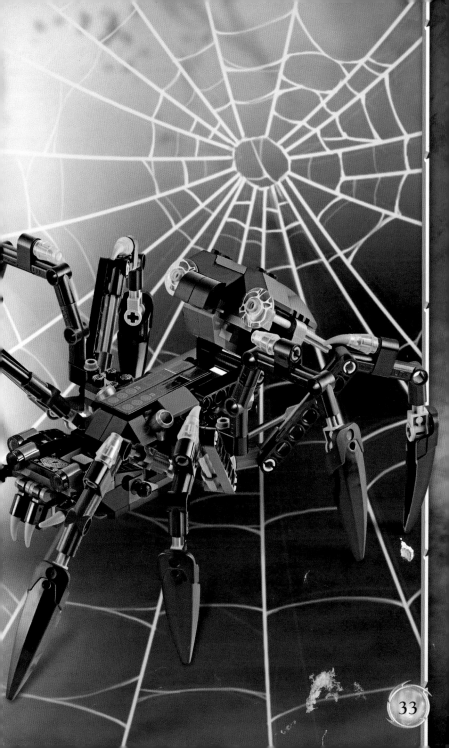

The Scorpion Tribe

The Scorpions are the most powerful of the Outland Tribes. Scorpions come in three ranks: the king, Stompers and Scrappers. Stompers are big, black scorpions who walk on six legs. The king wears gold armour and walks on two legs. Scrappers are small foot soldiers.

The Scorpions use their tails for clubbing and stinging. Stompers can even shoot poison from their tails!

The scorpion king is called Scorm. He is power-mad and gets angry very easily. Scorm wants all of the CHI for himself.

Scorpion Stinger

The Scorpion Assault Vehicle is a mean machine that attacks with its massive claws and pincers. Three wheels help keep it balanced so that it does not topple over.

The Stinger's tail jabs up and down to try and sting its enemies. The tail also shoots toxic "VenomBalls". Powerful pincers on the mouth crush anything in their way.

The Scorpion pilots sit in the cockpit and steer the Stinger into battle. The VenomBalls are loaded on the side, ready to be used against the enemy.

THE OUTLANDER MEETS THE ALMIGHTY
KING SCORM

EXCLUSIVE INTERVIEW

MEET THE
WONDERFUL
AND **INSPIRING**
LEADER OF THE
SCORPIONS.

Q Hello Scorm, we are big fans of yours, what have you been up to?

A I have been very busy making plans for world domination.

Q And what ' these plans involve?

A I need to capture all of the CHI from the Chima Tribes so that the glorious Scorpion Tribe can take their rightful place as leaders.

Q That sounds fantastic, and how lucky we are to have you as our leader.

A Yes, you are.

Q How do you manage to work with the Bats and Spiders?

A I am just using them to get what I want … I mean, what the Scorpions want, then we will not have to be allies with them any more.

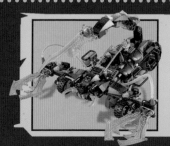

WHICH OUTLAND TRIBES ARE KING SCORM'S ALLIES?

Answer this simple question and win a chance to meet the King himself and ride his Scorpion Stinger.

The Bat Tribe

The Bat Tribe is the weakest and most stupid of all the Outland Tribes. Their strength lies in their numbers – there are hundreds of them!

The Bat Tribe is the only Outland Tribe that can fly. They use compact aircraft called Bat Flyers to penetrate the energy field around Mount Cavora. The Bat Flyers blow out menacing black smoke that surrounds Mount Cavora.

Bommerommer is the leader of the tribe. He will do whatever the Scorpions and Spiders tell him. His trusted assistants are Braptor and Blista. Braptor is the pilot of a powerful vehicle called the Wingstriker.

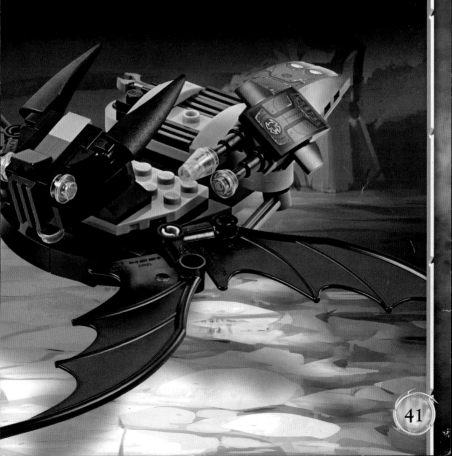

WATCH OUT!

A SURVIVAL GUIDE TO THE OUTLANDS

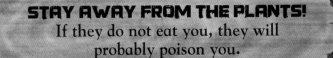

STAY AWAY FROM THE PLANTS!
If they do not eat you, they will
probably poison you.

DO NOT GET CAUGHT UP!
Watch out for the Spiders' deadly, sticky
webs. Once you are tangled up, you
will never get out.

HEADS UP!
Swooping bat clouds can
knock you off your feet.

KEEP YOUR BALANCE
The rocks in the Seesaw Valley sway
on top of towering spires and can
fall at any moment.

HOLD YOUR BREATH
Beware of the deadly fog
filled with toxic gas.

Gorilla Legend Beast

The Gorilla Legend Beast is bigger and stronger than Gorzan and his tribe. He is also gentle and loves having fun, just like Gorzan.

The band of heroes find the Gorilla Legend Beast first. They are relieved, but they have a difficult task ahead.

They have to first rescue him from the evil Spider tribe. He is caught in a huge spider web in the Spider canyon. The heroes disguise Rogon's truck as a big fly to distract the Spiders and free the trapped Beast.

Now, the heroes have hope. They can continue their quest to find the other Legend Beasts.

Eagle Legend Beast

The Eagle Legend Beast is a powerful bird of prey. She has huge wings, sharp talons and a strong beak. The Beast is very protective of her two eggs.

But, she is upset. The evil Outland Tribes have captured her eggs and trapped them on the Seesaw Rock. If the heroes are not careful, the eggs could slide off the slab and fall onto the jagged rocks below!

Eris rides on the back of the Eagle Beast to try and reach the eggs. Lavertus the Lion also comes to help on his WindShadow helicopter.

Eris puts her battle tactics to use.
Together with the band of heroes,
she finally manages to save the eggs.

Crocodile Legend Beast

The Crocodile Legend Beast is a strong swimmer and feels most at home in the water.

Like the other Legend Beasts, he is very big. Watch out for his shiny, white teeth – they are really sharp!

The Crocodile Beast likes Cragger. He lets him sit on his back and ride him across land or water. It is very useful when the heroes fall into a flooded canyon! Courageous Cragger rescues his friends by swimming out to them on the Crocodile Beast.

Wolf Legend Beast

The Wolf Tribe gives Worriz the special "Mother Tooth" charm to take on the quest. It will help Worriz find the Legend Beast. His tribe believes that the tooth belongs to the Wolf Beast. Worriz has a special connection with the Beast and is the only one who can understand his howl.

The Wolf Beast is trapped in the Scorpion cave. He has been put in a trance by Scorpion poison. Worriz uses the "Mother Tooth" to wake the Legend Beast from his trance.

The fierce Wolf Beast is very tough and once he is out of the trance, he easily escapes from the Scorpion cave.

Lion Legend Beast

The strong and noble Lion is the last of the Legend Beasts to be found. He is big and powerful with a thick brown mane and sharp claws. Laval decides to rescue him all by himself.

The Beast is trapped across a pool of water. Just like Laval, the Legend Beast is scared of water. He will not swim across the pool.

Laval overcomes his fear. He swims through the pool and helps the Legend Beast to swim back with him.

LEGEND BEAST AND LAVAL

SIMILAR YET DIFFERENT

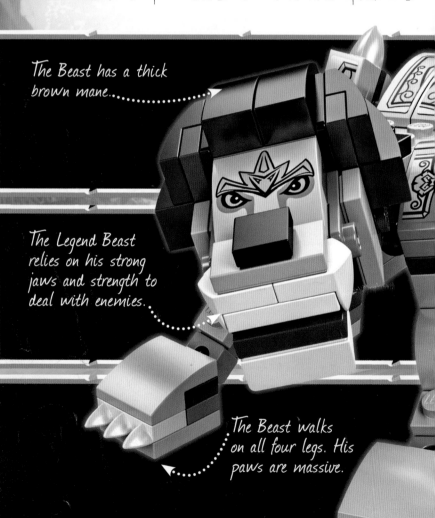

The Beast has a thick brown mane.

The Legend Beast relies on his strong jaws and strength to deal with enemies.

The Beast walks on all four legs. His paws are massive.

Laval loves a good adventure. The Lion Legend Beast is fierce and brave. What makes them a great pair is their love for Chima and their courage – they are both noble Lions. But, when it comes to size, the Legend Beast is a clear winner.

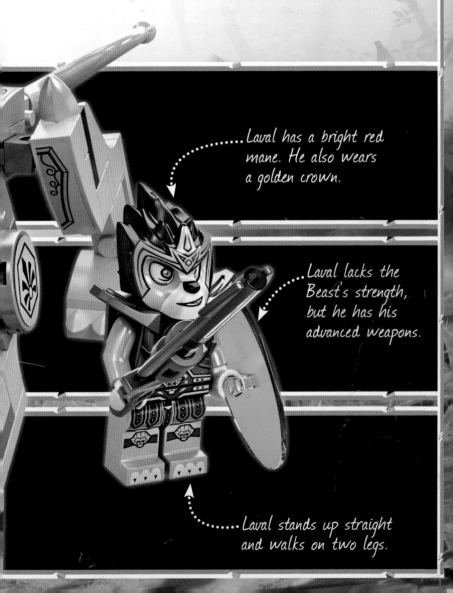

Laval has a bright red mane. He also wears a golden crown.

Laval lacks the Beast's strength, but he has his advanced weapons.

Laval stands up straight and walks on two legs.

Return to Chima

Victory! The heroes have finally found the Legend Beasts and defeated the Outland Tribes. Evil King Scorm vows to fight again when he gets more CHI. However, Laval gives Scorm the last orb of CHI. He explains that CHI must always be shared.

The heroes have survived the dangers of the Outlands. They return home to Chima, where the Legend Beasts magically fly into the waterfall caves of Mount Cavora. The water starts to flow again and CHI is restored to the Sacred Pool. The land of Chima and the animal tribes are saved!

Quiz

1. What is the name of the land that the animal tribes live in?

2. Where can you find the magical energy source known as CHI?

3. Who are the Band of Heroes looking for in the Outlands?

4. Who is Laval's father?

5. Who is Eris fond of?

6. What is Cragger the Crocodile's special weapon called?

7. Which of the Outland Tribes is the cleverest?

8. How do the spiders capture
   their enemies?

9. How many wheels does the
   Scorpion Assault Vehicle have?

10. What is the Lion Legend
    Beast scared of?

Answers on
page 61

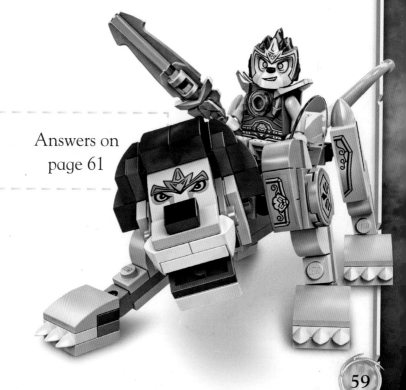

Glossary

determined
wanting to
do something
very much

domination
have power or
control over
someone or
something

headstrong
someone who
only does what
they want to do

mythical
existing only
in stories

menacing
a person or
thing likely
to cause harm

penetrate
to move into
or through

responsible
to have control
or be in charge

tactics
plan of attack

toxic
poisonous and deadly

trance
a dreamy state
where a person
does not know
what is going
on around them

vain
obsessed with your
own appearance

Index

Answers to the quiz on pages 58 and 59:
1. Chima 2. In the Sacred Pool 3. The Legend Beasts
4. King LaGravis 5. Rogon the Rhino 6. The Blade
Blaster 7. The Spiders 8. With their webs
9. Three 10. Water

Guide for Parents

DK Reads is a three-level reading series for children, developing the habit of reading widely for both pleasure and information. These books have exciting running text interspersed with a range of reading genres to suit your child's reading ability, as required by the school curriculum. Each book is designed to develop your child's reading skills, fluency, grammar awareness and comprehension in order to build confidence and engagement when reading.

Ready for a *Starting to Read Alone* book
YOUR CHILD SHOULD

- be able to read most words without needing to stop and break them down into sound parts.
- read smoothly, in phrases and with expression. By this level, your child will be mostly reading silently.
- self-correct when some word or sentence doesn't sound right.

A Valuable And Shared Reading Experience

For some children, text reading, particularly non-fiction, requires much effort but adult participation can make this both fun and easier. So here are a few tips on how to use this book with your child.

TIP 1: Check out the contents together before your child begins:

- Invite your child to check the blurb, contents page and layout of the book and comment on it.
- Ask your child to make predictions about the story.
- Chat about the information your child might want to find out.

TIP 2: Encourage fluent and flexible reading:

- Support your child to read in fluent, expressive phrases, making full use of punctuation and thinking about the meaning. Demonstrate this if necessary.

- Encourage your child to slow down and check information where appropriate.

Reading aloud is a way of communicating, just like talking and keeping a voice varied draws in the listener.

TIP 3: Indicators that your child is reading for meaning:

- Your child will be responding to the text if he/she is self-correcting and varying his/her voice.
- Your child will want to chat about what he/she is reading or is eager to turn the page to find out what will happen next.

TIP 4: Praise, share and chat:

- The factual pages tend to be more difficult than the story pages, and are designed to be shared with your child.
- Encourage your child to recall specific details after each chapter.
- Provide opportunities for your child to pick out interesting words and discuss what they mean.
- Discuss how the author captures the reader's interest, or how effective the non-fiction layouts are.
- Ask questions about the text. These help to develop comprehension skills and awareness of the language used.

A FEW ADDITIONAL TIPS

- Read to your child regularly to demonstrate fluency, phrasing and expression; to find out or check information; and for sharing enjoyment.
- Encourage your child to re-read favourite texts to increase reading confidence and fluency.
- Check that your child is reading a range of different types, such as poems, jokes and following instructions.

Here are some other DK Reads you might enjoy.

Starting to Read Alone

The Great Panda Tale
Join the excitement at the zoo as the staff prepare
to welcome a new panda baby.

African Adventures
Experience the trip of a lifetime on an African safari as recorded in
Katie's diary. Share her excitement when seeing wild animals up close.

Battle at the Castle
Through the letters of a squire to his sister, discover life in
a medieval castle during peacetime and war.

LEGO® Friends: Summer Adventures
Enjoy a summer of fun in Heartlake City with Emma, Mia,
Andrea, Stephanie, Olivia and friends.

Reading Alone

Terrors of the Deep
Marine biologists Dom and Jake take their deep-sea submersible
down into the deepest, darkest ocean trenches in the world.

Pony Club
Emma is so excited – she is going to horse-riding
camp with her older sister!

Star Wars™: Jedi Battles
Join the Jedi on their epic adventures and exciting battles.
Meet brave Jedi Knights who fight for justice across the galaxy.

Star Wars™: Sith Wars
Meet the Sith Lords who are trying to take over the galaxy.
Discover their evil plans and deadly armies.